Twelve Steps
To
BioFeedback
by George E. Soroka

Twelve Steps
To
BioFeedback

by George E. Soroka

All rights reserved.
Copyright ©1998 by George E. Soroka
Library of Congress Catalog Card Number: 98-92874
ISBN: 1-889122-24-6
Published by Ariel Starr Productions, Ltd.
P.O. Box 17 , Demarest, NJ 07627
Design and Layout by Creative Energy Enterprises, Inc.
For information on other books and audio tapes, write to:

George E. Soroka, Ltd.
"Twelve Steps To BioFeedback"
P.O. Box 242, Haworth, NJ 07641
email: GESoroka@aol.com
web: http://www.ceei.com/ges

PRINTED IN THE UNITED STATES OF AMERICA
This book is non-strippable
1st Edition - June 1998

<u>Dedication</u>

This booklet is dedicated to all whose goal is life itself, to the true friends along the way and to *Ben*, who is the true definition of 'Friend.'

Twelve Steps
To
BioFeedback
by George E. Soroka

step 1

We all have the problem of anxiety, fear, depression, difficulty in concentrating or a block to creativity. All of these can be summed up in one word: stress. Another word for stress is tension. There's nothing abnormal about stress or tension. But when these get in the way of living life to the fullest, then we should take a good look at them.

Twelve Steps
To
BioFeedback
by George E. Soroka

step **2**

What are the consequences of undue stress and tension? Recent clinical studies indicate stress and tension can significantly reduce one's life span. Witness the youngsters keeling over with coronaries, strokes and other diseases of older people. No one can effectively live his life under the cloud of high tension and stress. Productivity and creativity generally go down in direct proportion to the increase of tension and stress. Surely your own life should provide realistic support of the clinical evidence on undue stress and tension.

Twelve Steps
To
BioFeedback

by George E. Soroka

step 3

Over the past ten years, thousands of people have made the discovery of their lives. They have gained the ability to be in touch with themselves to such a degree that they are now free of the ill effects caused by fear, undue tension and high stress levels. This discovery came through the use of BioFeedback. First discovered at the Rockefeller Institute in 1967, BioFeedback is a proven form of self-communication. Remember what Shakespeare said, "This above all: to thine own self be true, and

Twelve Steps
To
BioFeedback

by George E. Soroka

step 3 continued

it must follow, as the night the day, thou canst not then be false to any man." BioFeedback starts an interaction between body and mind that gives you an inner calm you never knew before. BioFeedback is self-activating—once it starts working, it becomes like second nature to you.

Twelve Steps
To
BioFeedback
by George E. Soroka

step 4

W hat is the attractiveness of BioFeedback as a stress reducer?

a.   First of all, it works!

b.   It makes minimal demands on a person. While using the machine, you don't have to do anything. The miracle is that changes take place in you without you even trying. It just happens! Others notice you changing as well.

Twelve Steps To
BioFeedback

by George E. Soroka

step 4 continued

c. All that is required is a few hours per week for a six-week period.

d. It puts the individual in control again. You don't need a guru or a manual. Home is under your hat. It's like coming home again.

Twelve Steps
To
BioFeedback
by George E. Soroka

step 5

BioFeedback is an electronic monitoring of body stress and tension. It's comparable to putting a mirror before yourself. The stress is translated into an audio signal. What you hear is what you are at the present moment, in the here and now. If you are stressful and in tension, you know it!

Twelve Steps
To
BioFeedback
by George E. Soroka

step 6

What do you have to do? Three things only:

a. S T O P

b. L O O K   (observe)

c. L I S T E N   (to no one but you)

While on the machine, you stop and listen to yourself. While off the machine, you stop and look or observe your behavior during periods of stress. And you don't put yourself down when you get upset or flub something. You simply see it for what it is and go through it. You observe and you observe. But you do not judge yourself—or anyone else.

Twelve Steps
To
BioFeedback
by George E. Soroka

step 7

Here are some general principles that will help you understand BioFeedback:

a. The body has self-healing powers. Note what happens when you cut yourself. The wound heals ultimately. Doctors use drugs or surgery only to facilitate the natural healing powers of the body.

b. If you trust the body, it will bring itself into balance. Not trusting the body means using the mind to worry about the body,

Twelve Steps
To
BioFeedback
by George E. Soroka

step 7 continued

or even altogether ignoring the body and its danger signals.

C.   Man is made up of body and mind. We have stressed the mind to the point of making the body a stepsister. We almost wish our bodies away. We abuse them with drugs, overwork, tensions and stress. Sooner or later the body rebels and we have disease or imbalance in the body. Ever notice the Type "A," the

Twelve Steps
To
BioFeedback
by George E. Soroka

step 7 continued

workaholic or the stress-laden house-wife? They act as though they had no bodies. Then, when they get sick or have a coronary or stroke, they are forced to pay attention to the body—plenty of bed rest and so on. If only they had listened to the body earlier, they might have averted the collapse or disease. BioFeedback says: STOP, LOOK AND LISTEN! But now!

Twelve Steps
To
BioFeedback
by George E. Soroka

step 7 continued

d.   The basic urge of man is SURVIVAL.
      We want to extend life, to contribute to
      it and have the self space in which to
      grow. The human being uses two basic
      or rudimentary means for survival:

   FIGHT AND/OR FLIGHT

      The upper torso is geared toward fight,
      the lower towards flight. Arms are for
      fight and legs for flight.

e.   We become stress-full or tension-full

Twelve Steps
To
BioFeedback
by George E. Soroka

step 7 continued

when we think our survival is threatened in some real or imagined way. When we are under stress, our body gears up for fight or flight. The adrenaline pumps, our bodies sweat, our feet fidget, our arms become activated and we go through preparations for attack or retreat. We can feel our heartbeat quicken, our mouths get dry and our palms clammy. All of this is nature's way of helping us survive.

step 7

continued

when we think our survival is threatened
in some real or imagined way. When we
are under stress, our body gears up for
fight or flight. The adrenaline pumps, our
bodies sweat, our feet fidget, our arms
become activated and we go through
preparations for attack or retreat. We can
feel our heartbeat quicken, our mouths
get dry and our palms clammy. All of this
is nature's way of helping us survive . . .

Twelve Steps
To
BioFeedback
by George E. Soroka

step 7 continued

f. If we were living in a less civilized and educated environment, such as the steaming jungles of the Amazon, flight-fight responses would come in handy. We would react appropriately to an enemy that threatened our survival. But today, such drastic preparations on the part of the body are less than appropriate. A person's mind could tell him in an instant that survival is not threatened that frequently today.

Twelve Steps To BioFeedback

by George E. Soroka

step 7 continued

g. Despite this knowledge, most of us are in an almost perpetual state of flight-fight. And we are under incredible amounts of stress and tension. We can find justifications for our tensions, to be sure. But do they require the flight-fight response? Most of us are killing mosquitos with cannon fire. Our reaction is that ridiculous! For example, you go to speak before a group. Your heart pounds, you sweat, your voice cracks and you may

Twelve Steps
To
BioFeedback
by George E. Soroka

step 7 continued

even grow faint. Who is the enemy? Or
you go before an authority figure such
as a teacher or a policeman. Is he going
to kill you? And on and on it goes. You
have a fight with your spouse—you can't
even disagree without fight reactions.
You are contradicted and immediately
you lash out, ready to crush the enemy.
Know this much: all of this takes a toll
on the body and on life itself—it causes
a lot of dis-ease.

Twelve Steps
To
BioFeedback
by George E. Soroka

step 7 continued

h.   One reason we use the flight-fight reaction to such a degree is that a lot of us are immature. We are still babies, not adults. We think our survival depends on others. We still live in a crib and imagine that someone is going to steal our toys or not give us food. We relate as babies. Or else we relate as parents, trying to influence the survival of others, trying to control them. It can all be summed up by saying that we usually

Twelve Steps
To
BioFeedback
by George E. Soroka

step 7 continued

relate to others either by trying to control
them or trying to get their approval.

i. We should be neither child nor parent. We
should be adults. Being an adult means we
handle our own survival. Being a baby
means we are unwilling to accept responsibility for our own survival. Being a parent means we are unwilling to allow another to handle their own survival. When
we are not adults, we feel sick, so we give

Twelve Steps
To
BioFeedback

by George E. Soroka

step 7 continued

ourselves to another and say, "Make me well!" We demand that others save us thus putting an unfair burden on family, friends, religion, school and government.

j.   It is immaturity that makes us blame others for getting us upset. We evade responsibility. We exaggerate. We go into objection, and negate the goodness of life and reality. Immaturity, i.e., being a baby or a parent, means that our buttons can

Twelve Steps
To
BioFeedback
by George E. Soroka

step 7 continued

be pushed easily. We get bored easily. We
cannot be with ourselves. We cannot have
things the way they are. We have to control or to change things. We fidget, we
gossip, we wallow in tension and stress.
And we look for things outside of ourselves upon which to pin the blame for
our misery.

Twelve Steps
To
BioFeedback
by George E. Soroka

step 8

How does BioFeedback help a person become an adult?

a. You are trained to LISTEN to yourself. That tension registering on your machine is your tension. It is you! Be with it. Wear it. Feel it for what it is. Do not try to change it, to dump it on to someone else. That's your music. Face it!

b. Once you learn to stop resisting the machine, you discover that the body is more

Twelve Steps
To
BioFeedback
by George E. Soroka

step **8** continued

willing to communicate with you. Its sig-
nals become louder and more compre-
hensible. You begin to hear it saying:
SLOW DOWN. BE AN ADULT. BE
RESPONSIBLE. STOP BEING A
BABY! LET GO! STOP SEEKING AP-
PROVAL. LET GO OF WANTING TO
CONTROL! SURVIVAL IS OUR
BUSINESS—YOURS AND MINE!

C. When you are off the machine, you are

Twelve Steps To BioFeedback

by George E. Soroka

step 8 continued

asked to LOOK, to observe yourself and your behavior. Are you getting upset over nothing? Are you allowing others to push your buttons? Are you playing PARENT or BABY? And if you are not happy with what you observe, don't put yourself down. Don't punish yourself for not acting like an adult. EXPERIENCE THE WAY IT IS. It's all okay. Just go through it. Observe yourself, but do not judge! You'll do better without trying!

Twelve Steps
To
BioFeedback
by George E. Soroka

step 9

When you are off the machine, you can also get some good feedback. Next time you are on a train or in a group, look around you. Observe. See how the others are behaving. Note the feedback. That's how you are when you are under stress. You avoid another's gaze. Your head is drooped. Your shoulders sag. You carry the weight of the world around with you. You rush and you have to get where you are going—the harassed expressions, the bored eyes, the unwillingness of people to be

Twelve Steps
To
BioFeedback
by George E. Soroka

step **9** continued

with themselves and where they are.
Stress, tension, uptightness—you name
it—it's around you and in you. Is it all
worth the toll?

Twelve Steps
To
BioFeedback
by George E. Soroka

step 10

With BioFeedback, you begin to slow down, to enjoy life, to enjoy taking control of your own survival. You do not rush into things or away from people. And it's all automatic. You relax. And when you make a flub, you don't put yourself down. You observe and learn, always in control.

You STOP, LOOK AND LISTEN!

Twelve Steps
To
BioFeedback
by George E. Soroka

step 11

You change without changing your-self. It's natural. You find yourself more asser-tive and less aggressive. Who wants to fight? You are already in charge anyway. Your life is your own. Survival is in your hands. You are no longer bored. You like to be with yourself now. For you are in tune with yourself. Your body and your mind communicate. There is real dialogue. You have kicked the fear, anxiety and stress of yesterday.

Twelve Steps
to
Biofeedback

step 11

Twelve Steps
To
BioFeedback
by George E. Soroka

step 12

After awhile, you do not need the machine. You are naturally able to go with the motion of life. You no longer resist. And you are happier for it all. You can handle stress, tension and depression. You can face your fears and know that that's all they are. Really, BioFeedback is a route to your true Self!

WHY NOT TRY IT!
IT WORKS!

D.O.G./G.O.D.

ANOTHER QUALITY ENOCH PROJECT

D.O.G./G.O.D.

ANOTHER QUALITY ENOCH PROJECT